MY
PECULIAR

WON'T FIT IN A BOX

MARCIA BLANE, LPC

As we walk through various life experiences we often search for meaningful ways to share how those experiences make us feel. Unfortunately, we often run into situations where we have no one to listen to us, we are concerned about confidentiality or judgment, or we can't pull the words together to explain those experiences.

The Peculiar One guided journal encourages you to use pre-selected topics to begin writing about your journey. Your journey is unique and peculiar to you. You never have to fit in someone else's box. Create your own.

Happy Journaling,

Marcia

you are wonderful in your peculiar space

Happiness.....

Trying to find happiness can be a difficult journey but rewarding once we capture it. In this section, discussing what happiness looks like for you can open the door to your happiness. Only you have the right to define what happiness means to you. You are the key to your happiness, unlock it.

Grab your Happy,

Marcia

Wherever you go, no matter what the weather, Always bring your own sunshine

ANTHONY J. D'ANGELO

Define what happiness means to you.

Happiness is...

_____

_____

_____

_____

_____

_____

_____

_____

_____

_____

If you were able to create your space of happiness what would it look like?

My happy space looks like _____

_____

_____

_____

_____

_____

_____

_____

_____

_____

_____

_____

_____

you are wonderful in your peculiar space

What is stopping you from experiencing happiness?

_____

_____

_____

_____

_____

_____

_____

_____

_____

_____

_____

_____

you are wonderful in your peculiar space

We know every day isn't perfect. List what went right, what went wrong, and what changes would you like to see?

What went right?

_____

_____

_____

What went wrong?

_____

_____

_____

What would you change?

_____

_____

_____

_____

_____

_____

you are wonderful in your peculiar space

Your Happy Things

List 5 things that make YOU happy. Try to be selfish in your thoughts. Be Intentional when listing what makes you happy.

_____

_____

_____

_____

_____

_____

_____

_____

_____

_____

_____

you are wonderful in your peculiar space

You made it through the happiness section. On this page journal what you discovered about yourself. What adjustments are you making?

_____

_____

_____

_____

_____

_____

_____

_____

_____

_____

_____

you are wonderful in your peculiar space

Self-Validation / Self-Worth

There are negative individuals who pride themselves on bringing others down. Many of us have brought into the theme of not being enough. Being devalued by others is a heavy weight and regaining your power over the negative words is vital to experiencing joy, self-worth, and self-validation. Today is an opportunity to recontrol the power in us and reverse those negative words.

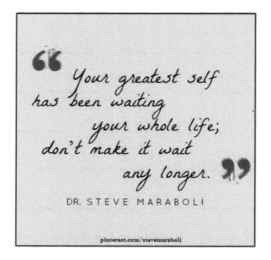

Your greatest self
has been waiting
       your whole life;
don't make it wait
       any longer.

DR. STEVE MARABOLI

pinterest.com/stevemaraboli

Your Younger Self

What would you say to your younger self?

_____

_____

_____

_____

_____

_____

_____

_____

_____

_____

_____

_____

_____

Self-Worth / Power Words

Identify and list words that are powerful and validating for you. It's time to take out the root of negativity using powerful words. Don't be shy, you are already awesome! Speak life into yourself!

_____

_____

_____

_____

_____

_____

_____

_____

_____

_____

_____

_____

Self-Love

Write 10 things that you love about yourself and why? (If you find it difficult to complete, no stress. Let it flow naturally and come back to it later.)

_____

_____

_____

_____

_____

_____

_____

_____

_____

_____

_____

_____

What is one negative thought that seems to never go away? Next to each negative word, change to a positive one. Let's change the narrative.

_____

_____

_____

_____

_____

_____

_____

_____

_____

_____

_____

_____

you are wonderful in your peculiar space

What is your natural gift!

_____

_____

_____

_____

_____

_____

_____

_____

_____

_____

_____

_____

_____

_____

The Person in the Mirror - Who are you?

Work on being in love with the person in the mirror who has been through so much but is still standing.

_____

_____

_____

_____

_____

_____

_____

_____

_____

you are wonderful in your peculiar space

Love Letter

Write a love letter to yourself.

_____

_____

_____

_____

_____

_____

_____

_____

_____

_____

_____

_____

_____

_____

_____

What did you learn about yourself in this section? What changes will you implement?

_____

_____

_____

_____

_____

_____

_____

_____

_____

_____

_____

_____

_____

you are wonderful in your peculiar space

Relationships

The value of relationship rests within you. The most important relationship you can have is the one with yourself. Learning who you are, what you like, and ignoring what others have tried to tell you about yourself will help you to walk in self-love.

Self-love is not selfish; you cannot truly love another until you know how to love yourself.	Work on being in love with the person in the mirror who has been through so much but is still standing.

Repeat this statement

I love the person that I have become in spite of what I have gone through. I value my existence and I treat myself like royalty.

What is your current relationship with yourself? Be truthful with yourself. What would you change?

_____

_____

_____

_____

_____

_____

_____

_____

_____

_____

_____

_____

Relationship Building

Everyone has a dream of what a relationship looks like.
What does your perfect relationship look like?

_____

_____

_____

_____

_____

_____

_____

_____

_____

_____

_____

What shaped or influenced your idea of a perfect relationship?

_____

_____

_____

_____

_____

_____

_____

_____

_____

_____

_____

_____

you are wonderful in your peculiar space

What characteristics of a perfect relationship do you bring to the table?

_____

_____

_____

_____

_____

_____

_____

_____

_____

_____

_____

_____

_____

_____

_____

_____

you are wonderful in your peculiar space

Write an introductory letter to your future mate.

_____

_____

_____

_____

_____

_____

_____

_____

_____

Free yourself from past relationship hurts.
Write down those hurts and on the next
page you will write down victories.

_____

_____

_____

_____

_____

_____

_____

_____

_____

_____

_____

List your victories from past relationships including the hurt and lessons learned.

_____

_____

_____

_____

_____

_____

_____

_____

_____

_____

_____

_____

you are wonderful in your peculiar space

What did you learn about yourself and relationships?

_____

_____

_____

_____

_____

_____

_____

_____

_____

_____

_____

_____

Forgiveness/Self-Forgiveness

One of the toughest things in life to do is to forgive. You often hear others say forgive but don't forget or I'll forgive over my dead body. I challenge you to look at forgiveness from a different lens. When you look at forgiveness as a way to release yourself from those that have hurt you, it empowers you to rebuild your life. The only person that you can control is yourself. The person that hurt you may or may not be aware of their hurt. Identifying your strength in forgiveness is your power. Forgiveness does not require you to have a relationship with the person that brought you pain. It allows you to discover your freedom to live. It allows you the right to choose peace and happiness. Forgiveness isn't a sign of weakness but one of strength and self-love. Let's journey into forgiveness.

What is the one thing that you haven't forgiven yourself for? What's holding you hostage?

What or Who is the person that you haven't forgiven? What's holding you up?

---

you are wonderful in your peculiar space

How has unforgiveness impacted how you have a relationship with yourself and others?

_____

_____

_____

_____

_____

_____

_____

_____

_____

_____

_____

_____

_____

Gratitude

"Gratitude is a powerful process for shifting your energy and bringing more of what you want into your life. Be grateful for what you already have, and you will attract more good things," -The Secret

How do you define gratitude or being grateful?

_____

_____

_____

_____

_____

_____

_____

_____

_____

_____

_____

Be in the moment! Right now, in this present space, write what you are grateful for.

_____

_____

_____

_____

_____

_____

_____

_____

_____

_____

_____

Challenges are to strengthen you. When you think of gratitude what challenges have you learned to be grateful for?

Be grateful for the small things. What are the small things in your life?

_____

_____

_____

_____

_____

_____

_____

_____

_____

_____

_____

_____

you are wonderful in your peculiar space

Be grateful for past experiences even those that left you hurt. What are some of those experiences? How have they shaped you?

_____

_____

_____

_____

_____

_____

_____

_____

_____

_____

_____

_____

_____

_____

I am grateful for my present experiences (list them), why?

_____

_____

_____

_____

_____

_____

_____

_____

_____

_____

_____

_____

_____

you are wonderful in your peculiar space

I am grateful for my future experiences (think out of the box).

No one knows what the future holds but turn gratitude on to manifest your desires.

_____

_____

_____

_____

_____

_____

_____

_____

_____

_____

_____

Moving into a place a gratitude allows you to experience things that are uncomfortable, but it encourages you to keep moving and expecting the good things.

Write about your experience through the gratitude section.

_____

_____

_____

_____

_____

_____

_____

_____

_____

_____

_____

Peace

The boundaries you establish outlines your peace. Finding peace is a selfish act that grants you the opportunity to participate in life's changes. The pursuit of peace gives you permission to experience life the way you choose. Living in peace allows you to move beyond fears and walk in power. Peace I bid to you.

Define what peace means to you.

_____

_____

_____

_____

_____

_____

_____

_____

_____

_____

_____

_____

_____

you are wonderful in your peculiar space

What boundaries have you put in place to keep your peace?

_____

_____

_____

_____

_____

_____

_____

_____

_____

_____

_____

_____

_____

_____

What barriers to your peace have you identified and how are you changing their power?

_____

_____

_____

_____

_____

_____

_____

_____

_____

_____

_____

_____

_____

_____

Don't Let People
Pull You Into Their Storms...

Pull Them Into Your Peace

Choose peace!

List some things that you can do when you feel that your peace is being pulled.

_____

_____

_____

_____

_____

_____

_____

_____

_____

Write a Peace statement.

_____

_____

_____

_____

_____

_____

_____

_____

_____

_____

_____

_____

you are wonderful in your peculiar space

If we have a positive mental attitude, then even when surrounded by hostility, we shall not lack inner peace.

_____

_____

_____

_____

_____

_____

_____

_____

_____

_____

_____

Write positive affirmations to yourself.

_____

_____

_____

_____

_____

_____

_____

_____

_____

_____

_____

_____

_____

you are wonderful in your peculiar space

Let your feelings flow! Write what comes to mind.

_____

_____

_____

_____

_____

_____

_____

_____

_____

_____

_____

_____

_____

you are wonderful in your peculiar space

Peculiar One Guided Journal is intended to help you journal life challenges, its goodness, and self-love. Finding your words through pain and joy can help empower your journey. If you found yourself uneasy or feeling like you need to talk more about a situation please contact a local therapist for assistance.

Remember you are your greatest asset!

Marcia Blane, LPC

www.peculiar1.com

you are wonderful in your peculiar space

CPSIA information can be obtained
at www.ICGtesting.com
Printed in the USA
LVHW020033170620
658107LV00012B/637